101 FUNNY JOKES

VOL. 1

THE HENNESSY KIDS

Featured Artwork by
ZOE TRAPPIER

The Hennessy Entertainment
Company

101 Funny Jokes / by The Hennessy Kids

ISBN 978-1-9994854-4-3 (Print)

ISBN 978-1-9994854-5-0 (E-book)

1. Wit and humor, Juvenile. 2. English wit and humor. I. The Hennessy Kids, author

The Hennessy Entertainment Company | HennessyEnt.com |

For all our friends who make us laugh!

1

FUNNY FOOD

What is a robot's favourite snack?
    Computer chips.

What do you call a fake noodle?
    An impasta.

What jam can't be eaten on toast?
    A traffic jam.

What kind of key opens a banana?
    A monkey.

Where do cannibals eat when they are on a car trip?
    Wherever they serve truck drivers.

Why did the cannibal spit out the clown?
    Because he tasted funny.

The cannibal child was too late for supper.
    His dad said, "Sorry, everyone's already eaten."

Which bean do kids like best?
    The jellybean.

What cake do you use when you want to clean your plate?
    A sponge cake.

The nervous sword swallower went on a diet.
    He was on pins and needles for months.

What kind of berry would you use with a colouring book?
    A crayon-berry.

What did the nut say when it got a cold?
    Cashew.

Why did the man stop working at the orange juice shop?
> He couldn't concentrate.

Did you hear the rumour about butter?
> I'll tell you if you promise not to spread it.

What did the hamburger name his daughter?
> Patty.

Did you hear about the race between the lettuce and the tomato?
> The lettuce was a head, but the tomato was trying to ketchup.

Why did the woman start a pizza shop?
> She wanted to make some dough.

I was so hungry at seven fifty-nine that I eight o'clock.

Let minnow if you can think of a good fish pun.

Why did the guy take a bath in vegetable oil?
> He wanted to wake up oily in the morning.

Why did the baby strawberry cry?
> Because his family was in a jam.

What the favorite fruit of twins?

    Pears.

What do you call a pea who didn't get enough sleep?

    Grum-pea.

2

WHACKY WORDPLAY

What's the hottest letter in the alphabet?
   B. You add it to oil and it makes it boil.

What is the longest word in the dictionary?
   Smiles starts with an s, ends with an s, with a mile in between.

Did you know there used to be only 25 letters in the alphabet?
   Nobody knew why.

What starts with a p, ends with an e, and has a million letters in it?
   Post office.

What race is never run?
A swimming race.

What has four wheels and flies?
A garbage truck.

What is the tallest building in the world?
The library. It has the most stories.

What has three letters and starts with gas?
A car.

Did you know each day starts with destruction?
The day breaks at the crack of dawn.

What has many teeth but cannot chew?
A comb.

Why won't a bicycle stand up when it's not moving?
It's too tired.

Why can't your nose be 12 inches long?
If it was 12 inches long, then it would be a foot.

What is the center of gravity?
    The letter V.

How do you make a pirate angry?
    Take away the p.

3

NATURALLY FUNNY

What is the most magical dog?
  A labracadabrador.

Which dinosaur gets into car accidents?
  Tyrannosaurus wrecks.

What sound do porcupines make when they kiss?
  Ouch.

What do you call a dinosaur when it's asleep?
  A dino-snore.

What goes meow-meow-meow-meow-meow-meow-meow-meow in the ocean?

An octo-puss.

What is the biggest ant in the world?

An eleph-ant.

What do you call a sleeping bull?

A bulldozer.

What kind of bird hangs out with a bulldozer?

A crane.

Why do seagulls only fly over the sea?

If they went across the bay, then they would be bagels.

Why do birds fly south for the winter?

It is easier than walking.

Where do sheep get haircuts?

At the baa-baa shop.

What's the most musical pet?

A trum-pet.

Did you hear that 1,000 hares escaped from the rabbit farm?
    Police are combing the area.

How do you make a skunk stop smelling?
    Give it nose plugs.

Why are some fish at the bottom of the ocean?
    Because they dropped out of school.

What did the buffalo say to his son when he dropped him off at school?
    Bison.

Why do bees have such sticky hair?
    Because they love their honeycomb.

How do you make an octopus laugh?
    With ten-tickles.

What bug is welcome in apartments?
    Ten-ants.

Why do tigers have stripes?
    So they don't get spotted.

Where do young cows eat at school?
   At the calf-eteria.

What do you call bears with no ears?
   B.

What is a bunny's motto?
   Don't worry, be hoppy.

How do rabbits travel?
   By hareplane.

How much space do fungi need to grow?
   As mushroom as possible.

How do trees get on the internet?
   They log on.

4

ARTWORK

WE ARE EXCITED AND HAPPY TO SHARE DRAWINGS SENT TO US FROM ZOE TRAPPIER!

Drawing by Zoe Trappier. Who is your Bee-F-F?

Drawing by Zoe Trappier.

PORK YAPINE

Drawing by Zoe Trappier. What do porcupines say when they kiss? Ouch.

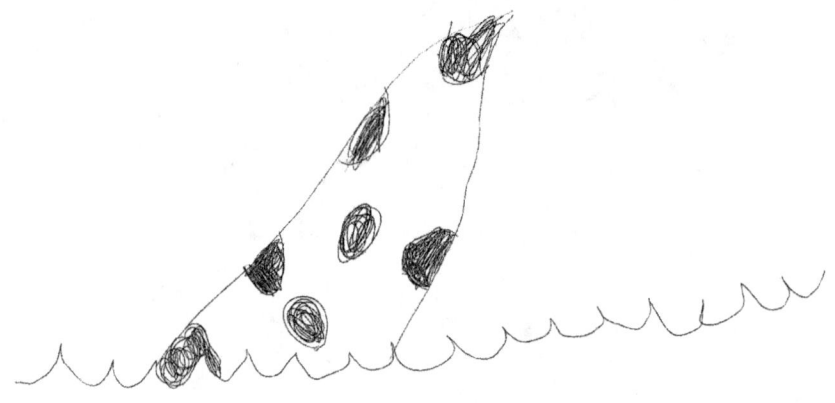

Drawing by Zoe Trappier. Would you swim with a pizza shark?

5

JOKEY JOBS

What did the dentist get for an award?
   A little plaque.

When time do most people remember to go to the dentist?
   Tooth-hurty.

Why did you handcuff the piano player's hands behind his back?
   To see if he could play by ear.

Why did the gardener bury her wallet in the ground?
   She wanted the soil to be rich.

What amazing luck! A writer dropped five stories into a garbage can and walked away unhurt.

Which month do soldiers hate most?
    The month of March.

Why did the robber take a bath?
    He wanted to make a clean getaway.

When do doctors get cranky?
    When they run out of patients.

Why did the person quit their job as an origami teacher?
    Too much paperwork.

What is a pirate's favourite letter?
    Arrrrr.

Why did the pirate pay two dollars to get his ears pierced?
    He was a buck an ear.

Why couldn't the pirate play cards?
    Because he was sitting on the deck.

Why couldn't the ten-year-old go see the pirate movie?
     Because it was rated arrrrr.

What did the pirate say on his 80th birthday?
     Aye Matey!

How did the barber win the race?
     With a short cut.

What sport are hairdressers great at?
     Curling.

What's an astronaut's favourite candy?
     A Mars bar.

Where do astronauts leave their spaceships?
     At parking meteors.

How do you make an astronaut's baby fall asleep?
     You rocket.

How do astronauts serve dinner in outer space?
    On flying saucers.

What kind of music do astronauts listen to?
    Neptunes.

6

SILLY SCIENCE

How does a scientist freshen her breath?
    With experi-mints.

What kind of flower creates electricity?
    A power plant.

Do you have dead batteries to give away?
    Yes, they are free of charge.

What kitchen appliance washes up on very small beaches?
    Microwaves.

Did you hear about the piece of wood that was grounded?
    It was bored.

Why is 6 afraid of 7?
>   Because 7 ate 9.
>   Why did 7 eat 9?
>   He wanted to have 3 squared meals a day.

The police are chasing the hacker.
>   Witnesses said he went data way.

I asked my librarian where I could find books on electricity.
>   She asked, "Current events or light reading?"

Where does bad light go?
>   Prism.

What did the volcano say to her husband?
>   I lava you so much.

Which kind of scientist should get more sun?
>   A paleontologist.

Did you hear thunder and lightning in the school science lab?
>   The students were brainstorming.

Why can you never trust atoms?
    They make up everything.

Where are the smartest trees found?
    In the brainforest.

What will go viral no many how popular it gets?
    Antibiotics.

Why did the cloud date the fog?
    He was so down to earth.

What does a cloud wear under his pants?
    Thunderwear.

Where do geologists sit to relax?
    In a rocking chair.

What's a math teacher's favorite tree?
    Geometry.

Why did the scientist read the book on helium in one night?
    She couldn't put it down.

How do you throw a party in space?
>You planet.

Why did the scientists take out their doorbells?
>They wanted to win the no-bell prize.

7

ACTIVITIES

READY TO GIVE YOUR MIND A WORKOUT?

HERE IS A MAZE, A NUMBER PUZZLE, AND A WORD SEARCH FOR FUN!

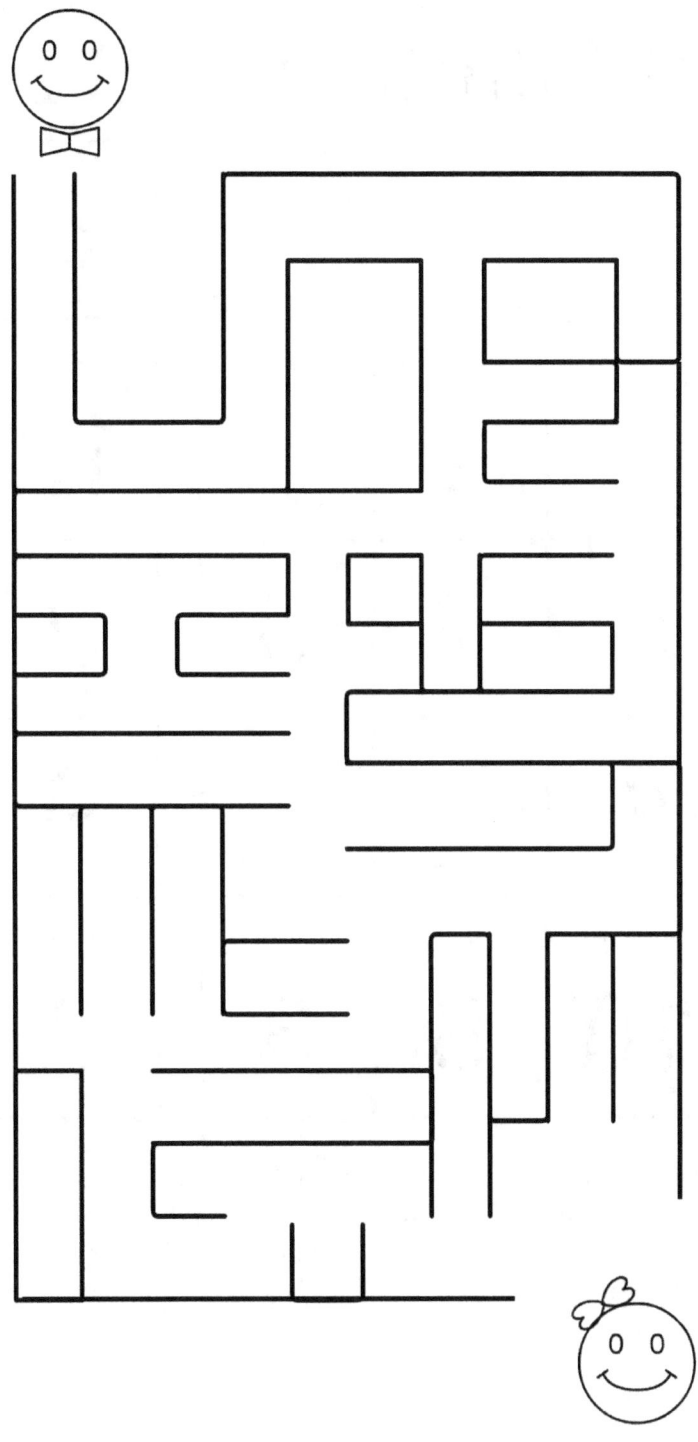

NUMBER PUZZLE

	8

	2		10
0	2	0	2
4		1	9

10	8	3	9

Missing numbers are between 0 to 9.
The numbers in each row add up to total on right.
The numbers in each column add up to total on bottom.
The diagonal numbers also add up to boxes on right side.

WORD SEARCH

```
Y  S  N  S  K  Y  R  A  K  A  R  N  P  F  U
U  E  N  P  E  K  C  A  E  Z  F  B  T  K  C
A  D  Q  O  L  I  T  C  Y  Z  L  Q  N  T  S
L  X  N  W  O  H  T  T  Y  I  E  T  O  W  K
I  D  N  O  E  D  W  S  B  P  U  R  H  E  L
H  V  C  R  F  B  L  E  E  X  M  W  J  E  O
C  R  I  K  H  A  L  E  D  B  A  Z  I  U  G
X  N  M  B  N  L  W  M  O  O  S  N  R  L  X
E  D  T  G  A  K  J  E  O  Z  A  N  U  O  X
S  L  W  Z  R  B  B  U  V  D  H  M  B  A  B
N  E  D  A  A  E  O  E  D  R  A  U  Y  E  S
J  P  H  Y  R  M  L  C  J  E  R  A  E  X  O
A  S  D  L  R  W  C  C  A  I  R  S  K  K  S
E  N  I  P  U  C  R  O  P  J  Y  Y  A  J  Q
W  Q  S  C  F  P  D  J  K  N  G  P  P  P  Y
```

AADEN	KHALED
BEES	KYRA
BELLA	NOODLE
BESTIES	PIZZA
DANIEL	PORCUPINE
HARRY	RUBY
JACOB	SAMUEL
JEB	SHARK
JUDE	ZOE
KATHERINE	

8

YOUR FAVOURITE JOKE

What is your favourite joke that isn't in this book?

Send it to us at thehennessykids@gmail.com, and we'll look to share it online with all our friends!

ACKNOWLEDGMENTS

Special thank you to Zoe Trappier, for sharing her drawings with us!

Thank you for reading our book! We hope you enjoyed it.
Please tell these jokes to your friends and family and make more
people happy.

ABOUT THE AUTHORS

The Hennessy Kids think the world would be better with more smiles.

Want to know when our new books and games are available? Sign up for our newsletter or visit www.hennessyent.com!

BOOKS BY THE HENNESSY KIDS

101 Funny Jokes, Vol. 1

101 Funny Jokes, Vol. 2

101 Pet Jokes

101 Knock Knock Jokes, Vol. 1

101 Knock Knock Jokes, Vol. 2

101 Knock Knock Jokes, Vol. 3

The Big Book Of Jokes

101 Nature Jokes

101 Food Jokes

101 Halloween Jokes

101 Christmas Jokes

101 School Jokes

Visit hennessyent.com for the complete up-to-date list of our books and games!